BLOOD OF THE SUN

Nov. 28, 2012

To Jim,
   Who slaughtered me at chess
(in the true world of the imagination)

      great visit— thanks
      a lot — um abraço,

More poetry by Salgado Maranhão
Punhos da Serpente
Palávora
O Beijo da Fera
Mural de Ventos
Solo de Gaveta
A Pelagem da Tigra
A Cor da Palavra

More works in translation by Alexis Levitin
Soulstorm by Clarice Lispector
Dark Domain by Eugénio de Andrade
New from the Blockade and Other Poems by Egito Gonçalves
Forbidden Words: Selected Poetry of Eugénio de Andrade
Guernica and Other Poems by Carlos de Oliveira
Cage by Astrid Cabral
Memory of Another River by Eugénio de Andrade

BLOOD OF THE SUN

SALGADO MARANHÃO   POEMS

Translated from the Portuguese by Alexis Levitin

milkweed
editions

Published 2012 by Milkweed Editions
Originally published 2002 as *Sol Sangüíneo* by Imago, Rio De Janeiro
Printed in Canada
Cover design by Hopkins/Baumann
Author illustration by Hopkins/Baumann
Interior design by Hopkins/Baumann
The text of this book is set in Bodoni Book with Bodoni Bold.
12 13 14 15 16   5 4 3 2 1
First Edition

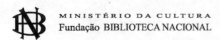

MINISTÉRIO DA CULTURA
Fundação BIBLIOTECA NACIONAL

This work published with the support of the Brazilian Ministry of Culture
Fundação Biblioteca Nacional/General Department of Books and Reading.
*(Obra publicada com o apoio do Ministério da Cultura do Brasil/Fundação
Biblioteca Nacional/Coordendoria Geral do Livro e da Leitura.)*

Please turn to the back of this book for a list of the sustaining funders of Milkweed
Editions.

Library of Congress Cataloging-in-Publication Data

Maranhão, Salgado.
    [Sol sangüíneo. English]
    Blood of the sun : poems / by Salgado Maranhao ; translated from Portuguese by
Alexis Levitin. — 1st ed.
        p. cm.
    ISBN 978-1-57131-453-6 (alk. paper)
    I. Levitin, Alexis. II. Title
    PQ9698.23.A624S6513 2012
    869.1'42—dc23
                                        2012007804

This book is printed on acid-free paper.

To Luiz Fernando Valente

Contents

Adereços para um Eclipse   Ornaments for an Eclipse

Sangue feroz do tempo possuído.

Wild blood of time possessed.

—Sophia de Mello Breyner Andresen

Thank you to the editors of the
following publications,
in which many of the poems
in this collection first appeared
in English translation.

Bitter Oleander
BOMB
Connotation Press
Controlled Burn
Cream City Review
Dirty Goat
Faultline
Florida Review
Fourth River
Left Curve
Massachusetts Review
Measure
Metamorphoses
Osiris
Per Contra
Pleiades
Review: Literature and Arts of the Americas
Rosebud
Spoon River Poetry Review
Subtropics
Talisman
Turnrow
Words Without Borders
Xavier Review

BLOOD OF THE SUN

Sol Sangüíneo
(Terra chã)

Para Cineas Santos e Sérgio Natureza

1.

Voltar ao desolado abrigo
da terra
       chã.
Voltar aos limítrofes
da palavra (larva fulminante
e alarde) que assiste
da despensa
ao rapto da existência.

Voltar ao solo atávico
onde os loucos
          riem-se
à sombra da neblina.

E — bardo — romper
a borda,
       rasgar o hímen
da linguagem
          que capta
em sua teia
os inquilinos do assombro.

O que move a lenda
é o fulgurar do incêndio,
o raio invicto
a fecundar a pedra.

Falo do que se inscreve
no inabordável
como a lua no lago
          alada.

Blood of the Sun
(Flat Lands)

For Cineas Santos and Sérgio Natureza

1.

To return to the desolate shelter
of the flat
            lands.
To return to the borders
of the word (larva ravenous,
a repressed roar) that witnesses
from the pantry
the violation of existence.

To return to the atavistic soil
where madmen
                  laugh
in the shadows of the mist.

And — the bard — to break
the border,
            tear the hymen
of language
            that traps
in its web
the tenants of astonishment.

What moves the legend
is the fire's blaze,
the undefeated ray
fertilizing stone itself.

I tell of what is inscribed
on the unapproachable
like the winged moon lying
                        on the lake.

Falo do que fálam
caninos num tempo de *crotalus*.

.Voltar ao fulminante alarde
da palavra.

I tell of what the canines
tell in the time of *crotalus*.

To return to the ravenous
roar of the word.

2.

Minha terra é o nome
que desabotoa o indomável.

A palavra física
em meu uivo esventrado. Minha
terra é ter-
        me.

E urdir
—no capítulo da carne—
o sopro itinerante;

e arder
sob o sono do tempo
e sua lírica de escombros.

Recolhido às artérias
lúdicas
ouço cantar a memória
no *living* das lagoas secas.

Insular e ascética a semente
fugaz dos rastros
                me guarda
em seu enigma.

Longe
é a flor que fala à contenção
que transborda.
E ao cio homicida que o vento
escuta e cala.

Do cais rasurado de esperas
velam noites a terçar
atabaques.

Minha terra é minha pele.

2.

My home is the name
that blossoms the indomitable.

The physical word
in my disemboweled howl. My
home is to own
                    myself.

And to weave
—in a chapter of flesh—
the wandering breath;

And to burn
beneath the sleep of time
and its lyric of debris.

Withdrawn to playful
arteries
I listen to memory sing
in a living room of dry lagoons.

Insular and ascetic the fleeting
seed of markings
                    holds me
in its mystery.

Far off
is the flower that speaks of a restraint
that overflows.
And of a murderous lust to which the wind
listens, and then grows silent.

From the dock wiped clear of waiting
nights keep vigil to the clashing
of African drums.

My home is my skin.

Das rinhas
em que o sal
dá músculos à água

vieram o sol —
e o azeviche
conjugados à carne;
e vieram moendas de açúcar
e súplica;
e vieram demandas de açoites
e séculos
a desatar fonemas
à fervura.

A mim que cingiram caminhos
ao mar de
           antilhas laceradas.

From cockfights
in which salt
gives water muscles

Comes the sun —
and the blackest black
mated to the flesh;
and mills for grinding sugar cane
and men in supplication;
and impositions of the whip
and centuries
of untangling phonemes
to add to the boil.

To me with whom they sailed their way
to the sea of
            the Antilles, lacerated.

3.

Reconheço-me no branco
que agasalha o rastro
das palavras. No rumor
de sílabas que lavram
minha urdidura: o parto
a granel sem sigla
ou *made in...*

—Nascer foi domesticar
as pedras.

Lentamente a carne exorta
ao poema
sua memória de cactos.

Eis as palavras apreendidas
ao deserto; eis as falanges
que vicejam cicuta
sob as flores.

(Ó vertigem de espinhos!)

Cada sopro é a noite
a esgrimir
sua asa de estio; cada cio
é o alfabeto
que desata o gesto.

Minhas pernas grafam
a pátina morena dos rios
de água turvas. Os rios
(ruminantes) sujos de argila
e sede.

Algo a forjar-me
esta língua de prismas,
réstias que adensam
a face expandida do sonho.

3.

I recognize myself in the white
that welcomes the trail
of my words. In the murmur
of syllables that work
my woven cloth: a birth
like gathered grain without a monogram
or *made in…*

—To be born was to domesticate
the stones.

Slowly the flesh exhorts
the poem,
its memory of cactuses.

Behold the words learned
in the desert; behold the fingers
blossoming poison
beneath the flowers.

(Oh the vertigo of thorns!)

Each breath is the night
fencing
with its wing of summer; each time of rut
is the alphabet
freeing gesture from its fetters.

My legs inscribe
the brown patina
of turbid waters. Rivers
(ruminant) soiled with clay
and thirst.

Something forging me
this language of prisms,
sheaves of light that thicken
the expanding face of the dream.

Ou sulcos no tempo
sem relevo: a goiv'arando
a névoa. E malho,
e lanho, e lírios insulares
ao olho—dardo à deriva—
de minha lavra de exílios.

Or furrows in days
without distinction: chiseling at
the mist. And maul
and lash and lilies like islands
to the gaze — a dart adrift —
labor of the exiled.

4.

Venho dos córregos
de água salobra,

do descampado
chão de farelos,

na cara o sol
rachou minha argila

seca: é o que digo
aos guardiões

que batem lata
em meu silêncio.

Distante ovulam
ritos na memória

como remendos
no ontem. E meu

olhar rasante
incide, infante,

ao *canyon* livre
e ao habite-se

da flama do dia
e sua *blitz.*

O que não busco
me tem

o que não houve
era meu

pedras no caminho torto
mentiras feitas de mel.

4.

I come from gullies
of brackish water,

abandoned fields
of stubbled earth,

the sun has cracked
the dry clay

of my face: that's what I say
to the guardians

rummaging about
in my silence.

In the distance, rituals
of memory ovulate

like patches
on yesterday. And my

sweeping gaze
swoops, a prince,

through the free canyon
and the dwelling place

of the flame of the day
and its blitz.

What I do not look for
holds me

what didn't exist
was mine

stones on the twisting path
lies made of honey.

Há que se viver o árido
como se cálido

há que se viver o breu
como se brio

há que se viver o nada
como se nada,
nada, nada até sangrar

que só dão água
para quem já tem o mar.

One must live the arid
impassioned and torrid

one must live the vile
with valor, with style

one must live nothingness
as if it were nothing,
nothing, nothing to the very last drop —

they only give water
to one who already has the sea.

5.

Êh mar, ímã de azuis, êh mar!
Linfa de sal (negreiro)
em minha carne
ciliar de palafita em flor.

Eis-me.
Cuspido ao pólen
da palavra,
minha terralenda
e súplica
que se exalta
no que em mim se inscreve
a barro
e sangue.

5.

Hey sea, magnet of blue, hey sea!
Lymph of salt (slave trade salt)
in the meat of my flesh
a circle of stilts in bloom.

Look at me.
Splattered by the pollen
of the word,
my legendland
and supplication
that exalts
what is written in me
in clay
in blood.

6.

As águas móbiles
                    do desejo
alçam-nos
à densa limalha dos dias,
ao voo das órbitas
                    submersas.

Urgem no átrio
em que a sede reincide: as
asas azagaias do desejo.

É sempre limiar o sol
que nos labora
                    o rito
da manhã
feita de azul e enzimas.

Assim as palavras
(que são flores de água)
alimentam-se de rimas
para entreter o vento.

Todas as coisas estão grávidas
de fogo. De um certo navegar
para nenhum cais.

Dentro de nós o tempo
seminal
          pagina a memória
anímica
como um deus que adoece.

Antes do que é brilho
e forma
a vida uiva para ninguém.

6.

The mobile waters
                    of desire
raise us
to the dense filings of the days,
to the flight of submerged
                                orbits.

They gather urgent in the atrium
where thirst repeats itself:
desire's two-edged sword.

It is always a threshold, the sun
that reinvents for us
                        the ritual
of morning
made of azure and enzymes.

That's how words
(flowers of water)
feed themselves on rhymes
to entertain the wind.

Everything is pregnant
with flame. With steady sailing
to no destination.

Within us seminal
time
        turns the pages of
anima's memory
like a god fallen ill.

Before there is light
and form
life howls for no one.

7.

O fogo infiltrado no olhar
amanhece
            o tecido da fábula,
exubera o sol
no gestual da noite
esquiva. A lágrima
rútila
que a manhã côa
do infinito ontem
                    espalha-se
na imensa teia de rasura
dos dias

ante o branco de nada
ante o branco mineral
de sal
            e silício.

E a boca espelha
a léria
            lúdica
onde tudo se esfarela
e a linha
            não alinha.

E nem a rinha
de extintores de sonhos
arrasa
        a fleuma
da palavra transfigurada.

7.

The flame that impregnates the gaze
gives birth to
        the woven tissue of the tale,
makes luxuriant the sun
as the night
slips away. The glistening
tear
that the morning distills
from infinite yesterday
           spreads itself
through the immense web of the erasure
of days

before the whiteness of nothing
before the mineral whiteness
of salt
        and silicon.

And the mouth mirrors
playful
       palaver
in which everything crumbles
and the line
       does not line up.

And not even the ring
of the destroyers of dreams
can annihilate
      the calm
of the transfigured word.

8.

Pelo menos resta
o verso — árido
mineral a soprar
sua luz transversa.

(E os remendos da linguagem
a despirem o que vestem.)

Abram-se talhos na tarde gris:
grafemas luminares.

No beco da página em branco
freme o lábaro do poema
ao rastilho de sílabas
cruas.

(Tão furtivo
que a palavra apenas
esmerilha
seu dorso de lince.)

Algo se rasga
na casca do insondável
(donde assisto ao tempo
atado à minha ínfima
espessura).

Algo marulha na derme
(e na calha)
do signo manifesto.

Minha terra é o nome
do indomável enigma:
a palavra física incrustada
na fábula.

Minha terra é minha pele.

8.

At least the verse
remains — arid
mineral breathing
its slant light.

(And the patches of language
stripping bare what they clothe.)

May the gray afternoon be rent:
luminary markings.

At the dead-end of the blank page
trembles the banner of the poem
to the trickling of raw
syllables.

(So furtive
that the word just
grazes
its lynx's back.)

Something is tearing
at the rind of the unfathomable
(where I attend time
tied to my minute
breadth).

Something is surging in the skin
(and in the furrows)
of the manifest sign.

My home is the name
of the indomitable mystery,
the physical word imbedded
in the tale.

My home is my skin.

TRIBES AND LITTLE SHOPS

(Tribos e Vitrines)

El poeta maldito
se entretiene tirándoles pájaros a las piedras.

—Nicanor Parra

Do arbítrio

Das estrias que a mão
esculpe
       só o que brilha
sobrevive.

Nômade a manhã
despe o sol
        à flor
da carne,

        múltipla,
à vertigem da linguagem.

Não há comportas
nem caminhos

não há saaras
nem vienas

em tudo há rinhas
e arestas
de flores
      e esquifes.

Em tudo entalha-se
ao revés
      coisas que se mostram
e não se dão,

que só no verso veem-se,
no *peeling* pelo avesso.

Of Will

Of the scratches sculpted
by a hand
            only those that glow
survive.

A nomad, morning
strips bare the sun
                    on the surface
of the flesh,

            multiple,
in the giddiness of language.

There are no floodgates
no paths prepared

no Saharas
or Viennas

in everything a battle
bedecked
with flowers
            and coffins.

In everything a carving
on the other side
                    of things that show themselves
but don't surrender,

that only are seen in a verse,
in the peeling of the underside.

(Delitos que em seu exílio
transbordam de rubro
                    a lira,
resenham através do júbilo,
rasuram através da ira.)

Sopra revanche de ritmos
no íntimo viés do não dito,

sopra o arbítrio dos dias.

(Offenses that in exile
drown the lyre
                    in ruby red,
record through jubilation,
erase through rage.)

The breath of rhythm's second chance,
the intimacy of unvoiced ways,

the breath of will, the breath of days.

Do sopro

O sopro que intercepta
o *self* dos meninos
                    avança
as águas turvas
e o rasgo
        da mirada.

(Límpido perfil do gesto
atado ao transe.)

O sopro lume
                e larva
pedra
        sangue
                flor

face ao que consagra
e nutre,
face ao vário
                desvario
onde anjos rotos
rezam aos abutres.
Há uma zona
em que os cristais
se partem
sob a lava ancestral
do sangue.
Há incêndios na raiz
do gesto. Vestígios
de pólvora nas palavras.
E quando há voz,
é a cicatriz que canta.

Of the Breath

The breath that intercepts
the selfhood of the boys
                        advances
turbid waters
and the tearing
            of a gaze.

(The limpid profile of a gesture
tied to their trance.)

The breath light
                and larval
stone
        blood
                flower

confronting what it consecrates
and nourishes,
facing the diverse
                the perverse
where tattered angels
pray to vultures.
There is a place
where crystals
fall apart
beneath the ancestral lava
of blood.
There is a blaze in the roots
of a gesture. Vestiges
of powder in the power of words.
And when there is a voice,
it is the scar that sings.

Das coisas

As coisas órfãs de luz
assaltam nossos azuis

dispersos. As peças vivas
—lavas de sombra à deriva—

zoam na humana paisagem
rente à linha de montagem

do desejo. (Ou cintilância
que o poder das coisas lança?)

Tralha que nos cerra os cílios
vida, loja de utensílios,

víveres. Onde outros rumos
aos que no tecido ousem

roer o fio de prumo
dos que de coisas se cosem?

Of Things

Things, orphans of light,
attack our little tithe

of sky—blue light.
Alive, they writhe

—lava of wandering shades—
buzzing through human glades,

a landscape of our kind,
reflecting the assembly line

of our desires. (Or is it shimmering
forth the very force of glimmering

things themselves?) Junk that seals our eyelids shut
our lives, department stores, that glut

of endless goods. Could there be another way
for those within the web to fray

the plumb-line, plunge a knife
into the fabric of our daily life?

Do espelho

Tons de íris lago furta-cor
de labareda sem o fogo

vero. A face plana e muda
mármore, inunda o que desnuda.

E do poder que serve ao extremo
de nos vender o que já temos,

reina o espectro volátil
das águas, que da pedra tátil

deságua. E a imagem em seu sê-lo
a tornar-se asas do espelho

que frio se acasala sem cio:
uma rima para silêncio.

Of the Mirror

Lake-iris iridescent hue
of flames that flicker without true

fire. Its surface smooth, serene, fair,
a marble face that floods what it strips bare.

The power, too, to sell or loan
us what already is our own.

Solid stone, it serves as host
to a governing shadow, a watery ghost.

That liquid image, though it flees,
wings the mirror with utter ease

to an icy coupling, devoid of heat:
a silent mating, without meat.

Do raio

Nem o acre sabor das uvas
nos aplaca. Nem a chuva

nos olhos incendidos
devolve o que é vivido.

O magma que nos evapora
tange o rascunho das horas

sob um raio de suspense.
Nem o que é nosso nos pertence.

Of Lightning

Even the bitter taste of grapes
does not appease us. Nor does rain

upon our burning eyes
return to us what we have lived.

The magma that consumes us
banishes our sketch of hours

beneath a bolt of lightning in suspense.
Not even what is ours belongs to us.

Da dor

Invicto
o coração
desata
incêndios

intacto
o estio
na carne
incrusta

até onde
é lanho
o exaspero

e a dor
servida
à la carte

no afã
de dar
ao verso
          víscera.

Of Pain

Unvanquished
the heart
dissolves
fire

intact
the summer
encrusts
our flesh

until
livid turns
to lash

and pain
is served up
à la carte

in its eagerness
to give
viscera
        to verse.

Da lâmina

Do silêncio da faca
que entre frutas medita
seguem-se alegorias
das artérias aflitas

que de susto vislumbram
o que na faca alude
em seu bote certeiro
em sua trama rude.

Do silêncio afiado
que na faca labute
decolam águas rubras
que se querem desfrute

da carne que lateja
seu líquido sanguíneo
a tornar-se erosão
sob o mesmo moinho.

Pois tudo reina a um triz
do corte cego no ar,
algo que se pressente
mas se busca olvidar,

o furor tão sutil
como o brilho de um quartzo
a lembrar que a partida
encerra-se num lapso.

Ardis, luares, tertúlias…
são só brechas no muro
da espera, ante o rilhar
da lâmina no escuro.

Tal como — ao quebra-mar —
sobre os frutos da pedra,
em seu tecido de átomo
a terra se desprega.

Of the Blade

From the silence of the knife
as it ponders fruit
arterial allegories
take anguished root.

In fright the fruit discern
the knife's profoundest theme,
the pinpoint thrust,
the scream.

From the keen-edged silence
gathered in the knife
crimson oozes forth
offering its life

for flesh that throbs
a blood-red moan,
ground beneath
its own millstone.

There's something we foresee, foreknow,
a blind slash hanging by a thread:
we're here by the skin of our teeth.
We'd like to forget our dread.

Violence as subtle
as quartz's glinting light—
a reminder that the game
ends with an oversight.

Tricks, moonlight, the usual crowd,
just cracks, rifts in the wall
that simply waits for the screech
that comes in the dark for us all.

Just as on the seawall,
beneath shell-crusted stone,
in its weave of atoms
the earth returns its loan.

Tal como a rede puindo
sobre um solo de farpas
e o prumo do equilíbrio
que o temporal desata.

Ou a frase em meio-tom
—entre o outono e a canícula—
tendo o enredo da vida
suspenso numa vírgula.

Or as a hammock frays,
slung over splintered ground,
and a delicately balanced scale
is crushed when the storm comes down.

Or a half-whispered phrase,
between dog days and the fall,
the plans we have for life —
a comma ends them all.

Do silêncio

Para Jorge Wanderley

Não precisa de nós
o silêncio:
já possui sua coda
de música
        muda:
secreta seita
em que se enreda
e se desnuda.

Não precisa do nosso
exaspero
nem do ruir
        das coisas
físicas
sujeitas à limalha
e à ferrugem.

—Cantar e esculpir
rumores.

Imerso em nossa espera
o silêncio nos arresta
        em sua forma
de estar ausente.

Of Silence

For Jorge Wanderley

Silence
doesn't need knots:
it already possesses its coda
of mute
      music:
secret sect
in which one is wrapped
and stripped bare.

It doesn't need
our rage
or the collapse
         of things
physical
subject to sawdust
and to rust.

—To sing is to sculpt
sounds.

Immersed in our waiting,
we're arrested by silence
          in its guise
of absence.

Do tempo

I

Decola dos dias ávidos
para o colo da sintaxe,
o ermo
            voo da língua
sob a voz. Pulsa
nos átrios
                a espessa urgência
da dor
no átimo que o tempo
inscreve
            o que nos ergue
e nos renega.

Pulsa a voragem
                    da chama
sobre a íris
no rastro que o tempo grafa
nossa incerta iluminura.

Of Time

I

Taking off from days avid
for the breast of syntax,
the lonely
flight of language
beneath the voice. There throbs
in the atria
            the thick urgency
of pain
in the instant that time
inscribes
            what lifts us up
and then denies us.

There throbs the voracity
                        of flame
pulsing the iris
the trail that time carves
our dubious illumination.

II

Devagar
as palavras amanhecem
para exaltar o que não fomos.

O poema se debate
entre pupilas,
dói no espelho,
dói no sopro e dói

onde a luz é pedra
onde o osso é uivo;

ruge sob as veias ocas
a resgatar o espectro
larvar
das palavras adormecidas; arrima-se

na lâmina
que se irmana
à possessão da vertigem.

O poema-carne,
cingido a pregos
e a tijolos crus,
arrebenta o mar
que nos inunda.

II

Slowly
words dawn
to exalt what we never were.

The poem struggles
among retinas,
aches in the mirror,
aches in the breath and aches

where light is stone
where bone is howl;

it roars beneath hollow veins
ransoming the larval
specter
of sleeping words; it leans upon

the blade
that couples
with the ecstasy of vertigo.

The poem-flesh,
bound with nails
and unbaked tiles,
breaks against the sea
that drowns us.

LOOM OF FEELING

(Tear dos Afetos)

*(Aliás
o engano, a ilusão,
a mentira, a falsidade,
o perjúrio, a invenção,
tudo, em Amor, é verdade.)*

(And so
deceit, deception,
lies, equivocation,
false promises, fairy tales,
all, in Love, is true.)

—António Gedeão

Limítrofe 1
(Cerco de vozes)

Quando o fogo rasgar
tua semente
        líquida
—e de mares forem tuas
leis—
guardarei o recorte
em meu pequeno cais.

(À parte o triunfo do ritmo
sobre o coração—naufragado
em seu ouro submerso—outro
é o veio
        anverso
a exortar
        o sol.)

Tudo zoa
tudo arrulha
para dentro do imprevisto,
como zine o azul
na memória.

Por isso
este cerco de vozes,
por isso esta armadura
ao cintilar de facas.

Sangue
é no que ardo
vívido de fonemas
e lascívia
sã.

Cingido a meu voo inacabado
o hoje é minha largura.

Boundary 1
(Circle of Voices)

When fire tears
your liquid
            seed
— and tides become your
laws —
I will keep your image
on my little quay.

(Apart from the triumph of rhythm
over the heart — foundered
on its submerged gold — there is
an obverse
            rivulet
exhorting
        the sun.)

Everything hums
everything coos
within the unexpected,
the way blue shrills
in memory.

Therefore
this circle of voices,
therefore this armor
facing the gleam of knives.

Blood
is where I burn,
alive with phonemes
and blessed
lust.

Bound to my unfinished flight,
today is all my breadth, my height.

Limítrofe 2
(Depois do inverno)

Depois que caírem
        —maduras—
as chuvas
      no barro
bárbaro,

relevos
     de tua presença
íngreme
sumirão nas águas
        loucas.

(Vestígios
     de tua voz
soletram marcas
       no dorso
dócil:

nada que a mão
possua
     dessa restinga
de desejo
    avaro.)

O branco enumera
o nada

e noutras marginais

  —revérbero do hospício
a pique—o coração
máquina
     impermanências.

Boundary 2
(After Winter)

After ripe
      rains
fall
   on savage
loam,

your steep
        sheer
silhouette
will disappear in
             maddened waters.

(Vestiges
      of your voice
spell out their markings
          on my docile
back:

there is nothing that my hand
possesses now
        of that salty marsh
of avaricious
     appetite.)

White recounts its
nothingness

and in others beyond the pale

—brilliance of the madhouse
as it founders—the heart
contrives
     impermanence.

Horas de litanias
e desenlace;
horas impermeáveis
—como a loucura—
desatam
     asas
no invertebrado
         voo
do fogo.

Hours of litany,
of letting loose;
hours impermeable
as madness
unfold
          their wings
in the invertebrate
                    flight
of fire.

Limítrofe 3
(Tear de afetos)

Floram
manhãs
sobre a caligem
            de argila
fundida
      ao vento.
Sopram rumores
da trama
       elástica
que se desata,
a comer hipóteses
a tingir meu sangue
em ciclos.

Da névoa
estende-se o cortejo
de vozes,
       o tear
de tessituras
ávidas.

O aço ríspido
que arrasa
      as flores
da canícula
não lacera a memória
do olho
nem as cores tangidas
ao informulado.
Apenas amanhece
         meu júbilo
com palavras.

Boundary 3
(Loom of Feeling)

Mornings
blossom
above the dust
               of dry clay
mixed
       with the wind.
Whispered rumors breathe
an elastic
               drama
that is slipping loose,
eating away at possibilities,
staining the cycles
of my blood.

From the mists
a procession of voices
stretches forth,
                    a loom
of anxious
weavings.

Crisp steel
that levels
               dog day
flowers
doesn't lacerate the memory
of the eye
or those colors banished
to the inchoate.
All that dawns
               is the joy I take
in words.

Denso é o silêncio
a inundar
    o que gela
e o que ruge.
Destro é o vento
(antiquíssimo)
que me assalta
para sua penugem.

Não cantarei no cais
a noite ininterrupta
nem terei corvos
        (de guarda)
à minha porta.

Anfíbio,
    sigo um tempo
que transmigra
a recolher tua ausência
pressentida.

Dense is the silence
drowning
            what freezes
and what roars.
Deft the wind
(ancient of ancients)
that draws me
to its down.

I will not sing upon the quay
uninterrupted night
nor will I welcome
                        guardian crows
before my gate.

Amphibian,
            I follow transmigrating
time
that gathers up your absence,
foreknown, forefelt.

Limítrofe 4
(Imaginário mar)

Impávido, o amor-
mor
    reedita
a fugaz simetria
dos corpos.

No *stand* do desejo
a mão hiberna
os frutos
        impalpáveis:

relíquias
que o olho cifra
no imaginário
          mar;

liquens
do salitre
      que escarna
a nudez
     de tudo
e
torna
o retorno
a zero
    —sem palco
    e sem plateia —

ou
sola e brilha
no imenso
     nada

como o ouro
das estrelas mortas.

Boundary 4
(Imaginary Sea)

Intrepid, greater-
love
    re-edits
the fleeting symmetry
of bodies.

In the showcase of desire
the hand hibernates
impalpable
        fruit:

reliquaries
the eye engraves
in an imaginary
        sea;

lichens
of sea salt
      that eat away the very flesh
of all
    our nakedness
and
turn
return
to zero
    without a stage
    without an audience

or
a solo sparkling
in the immensity
      of nothingness

like the gold
of stars long dead.

Limítrofe 5
(Ogivas)

Para Cacau

Teus olhos água lúmen
        na xícara de chá.

São duas ervilhas
              virgens:
tuas ogivas ágeis.

Falam pela córnea exilada
em mim

que rasga à flor do lábio
o hálito de pequenas
mortes.

Um a um, os teus gestos
grifam
        secretos acervos
mesmo quando púrpura
rosna
a cidade dos humores.

Agarro-me
        a teus capilares:
rotas de fuga
        e permanência.

A nudez nos aborda
nas entrelinhas
           tortas
e nos desacordes.

Livres do cerco de fogo
erguemos no pó
        nosso ramo de fábulas.

Boundary 5
(Warheads)

For Cacau

Your eyes water-lumen
                    in a cup of tea.

Two virgin
            peas:
warheads in flight.

They speak through the cornea exiled
in me,

that tears to the surface of my lips
a breath of little
deaths.

One by one, your gestures
underscore
                a stack of secrets
even when your city
growls
its purple humors.

I cling
        to your capillaries:
trajectories of flight
                        and permanence.

Nakedness approaches us
between our twisted
                        lines
and you untune us.

Free of the circle of fire
we raise from the dust
        our branch of mythic tales.

Limítrofe 6
(Degelo)

Ao resenhar teus remotos contornos
descubro alusões
                    pictóricas
—não a Renoir—
                    a Modigliani
e suas fêmeas
de longilíneos caules.

Textura estampada
em *ton sur ton*
as linhas de movimento
—em *allegro moderato*—
marginam teus frutos úmidos.

(E raia do triângulo oculto
o *design* despido
                    do *piercing*
em teu clitóris.)

Estão maduras as formas
nas entrelinhas
dos teus abismos,

nos entalhes que degelam
tua mobília de águas.

Boundary 6
(Thaw)

Recording the remote contours of your flesh
I discover pictorial
                              allusions
—not to Renoir—
                              but to Modigliani
and his females
with their long stretched stems.

Texture imprinted
en ton sur ton
the lines of movement
 — in *allegro moderato* —
delineate your moistened fruit.

(And glistening in the hidden triangle
the design, exposed,
                              of the piercing
in your clitoris.)

The shapes
between the lines
of your abyss are ripe

in the deep grooves that thaw
your wealth of waters.

Limítrofe 7
(Pó e reticência)

Que mares me adensam
para dentro

eu que me faço
à margem,

eu que renasço
do limbo

ao doce furor
das águas? Porosa

a boca — porto
de salina e sons —
abriga o voo
                sobre a seara
em que meus
                    pássaros
se aquecem.

Movam-se limítrofes
                    de mim
por onde a noite escreve
cicatrizes.

Somente os viajantes
                    sem morada
os cães filhos da lua
seduzem
            o abandono
e as distâncias.

Boundary 7
(Dust and Reticence)

What mounting seas are moving
me within

I who fashion myself
on the margins

I who am reborn
from limbo

to the sweet furor
of the waters? My porous

mouth — port
of salt and sounds —
harbors the flight
                    over grain fields
from which my
                    birds
take warmth.

My boundaries
                    move
toward where the night writes
scars.

Only travelers
                    without a home
and dogs, those children of the moon,
seduce
        solitude
and distances.

Nada a fazer do tempo
que nos olha o dorso
por entre ruínas
                    e espirais
de tílias.

Ante o que dói
e o que dorme:
apenas pó
e reticências.

Nothing to be done with time
watching at our back
among ruins
         and spires
of linden trees.

Before what suffers
and what sleeps
just dust
and reticence.

GRAY LEGEND
(Legenda Gris)

Lequel est l'homme du matin
et lequel celui des ténèbres?

——René Char

Fero

Tento esculpir a litania
dos pássaros
e as palavras mordem
a inocência. Aferram-se
ao que é de pedra
e perda.

(Canto ao coração e tudo é víscera
como na savana.)

Restolhos de espera
e crimes;
insights de insânia
e súplica; volúpias insolúveis
acossam-me a página
em branco
qual bandido bárbaro
ou mar revolto
a rasgar a calha
do poema.

Nada me resgata.
Não sei se sou quem morre
ou quem mata.

Rage

I try to sculpt the litany
of birds
and the words bite
innocence. They cling
to stone that lasts
and loss.

(I sing the heart but all is viscera
as on the great savannah.)

Residue of hope
and crime;
insights of insanity
and supplication; insoluble sensuality
surround the whiteness
of my page
like a bloody buccaneer
or raging sea
tearing at the pathway
of the poem.

Nothing ransoms me.
Am I the killer
or the killed?

Via crúcis

Ondas de ruídos
                    urdem
o *script*
        das ruas

(a fauna férrea
impera seus amperes).

Ondas de ruídos
ruem
        entre asilos
de pedra
e sons de
            sós
anônimos.

Rondam
—os autos
            e os bípedes —
no *drive-in*
        da via crucis.

Via Crucis

Waves of sound
               weave
the script
       of the streets

(unrelenting fire
feline ferocity).

Crashing waves of sound
collapse
           among sanctuaries
of stone
and sounds of
              solitary
anonymity.

They prowl about
—bipeds
       and their vehicles—
 the drive-in
       this, our via crucis.

Legenda gris

Outra lua se arma
nas esquinas —
                gris
— rasgada a sangue
e fuligem.

Outra luz fendida
em meus afluentes
          cedilha
na noite interdita.

E gane à foz
              do esgano
que a cidade acidula.

Ícones de cera
                  acercam
a metrópole das imagens,

no estábulo do mínimo/
máximo,

paralelos enredos
reescrevem o caos.

Passam latas voadoras
passam fantoches insignes
passa a manhã de raspão

no chão que a noite rubrica
suas estrelas de sombras.

Gray Legend

Another moon arms itself
on the corners of the street —

                             Gray

— torn and bloodied
and covered in grime.

Another cloven light
upon my tributaries
      a cedilla
in forbidden night.

Where the river empties a yelp

                                  of strangulation
that the city turns more bitter still.

Icons of wax
             surround
this metropolis of images,

in the stable of minimum/
maximum,

parallel plots
write chaos once again.

Pieces of junk fly by
illustrious puppets go by
morning itself scratches by

on a surface that the night initials
with its shadowy stars.

Mural

Para Armando Freitas Filho

Ali —
que a suástica morde
o muro —

em vez do belo,
bílis.
Alistam-se ao grafite
aflito
injúrias de cães enfermos.

Ali —
onde os rastros desembarcam
na borda de trilhos cegos —

confluem tempo
e esterco.

Ali
na chapa quente
na fímbria do escuro
no cimento cru.

Dias como se pássaro
séculos como se fóssil

aos que metem a ripa
aos clones de Judas
aos que alugam a tripa.

Ali
no rol do resto
no contrapé
no bote

onde a empáfia pifa
derrapa
stop.

Mural

For Armando Freitas Filho

There—
where the swastika wears into
the wall—

instead of style,
bile.
Aggrieved graffiti
list
the injuries of sickly dogs.

There—
where their tracks disembark
beside blind paths—

time and excrement
flow together.

There
on the burning grill
on the fringes of darkness
on raw cement.

Days like birds
centuries like fossils

before those who snap the whip
before the clones of Judas
and those who sell their ass.

There
in the rolls of the remains
the lowest prop
the sudden thrust

where aloofness goes poof
it slips, skids, slides
to a stop.

Pipoco

A cápsula de AR-15 rola no pó
sob a mira do tempo exausto. Remete
ao instante em que a pólvora desova o estampido:
a dose de fúria que deflagra o grito e o tombo.

A cápsula exposta ao alcance dos olhos e do susto.
E todo o eterno impresso num relâmpago.

Bang

The casing from the AR-15 rolls in the dust
beneath the gaze of exhausted time. It points back
to the instant when the powder spawned the sudden blast:
a dose of fury bursting forth, a scream, a dropping to the ground.

The cartridge casing naked to our frightened eyes.
And all eternity imprinted in a flash.

Execução

Projéteis latejam como gotas
de luzes inocentes,

no corpo ermo,
                    desabitado,
impróprio para o uso.

Ideogramas de sangue-flor
se vão cosendo no tecido
                              roto.
Na quilha exposta
à fratura

uma névoa da noite enluva o nada.

Execution

Projectiles pulse like drops
of innocent light,

in the body now deserted,
                              uninhabited,
unfit for use.

Ideograms of blood-flowers
sewing, sewing torn
                            tissues.
On the naked
fractured keel

night mist envelops nothingness.

O Açougue Nutriz

Dancei num matadouro, como se o sangue de
todos os animais que à minha volta pendiam
degolados fosse o meu
—Luís Miguel Nava

Assisto aos bois dependurados nos varais.
Assisto à solidão vermelha (aos pedaços) na
vitrine. O berro que (ainda!) respinga na pedra
lisa. E o espectro de anjos tatuados de sevícias.
Alastra-se a gula transeunte ante o rumor da
oficina de sangue nutriz. Esse sangue que em
nada se nos apieda (ou o instante em que a
faca sublima nossa porção coiote), recende em
nós as fibras da podridão impávida. Como se,
no íntimo, o açougue se despisse a esgarçar os
dutos por onde esguicha nossa santidade.

Wet-Nurse Butcher Shop

I danced in the slaughterhouse, as
if the blood of all the animals hanging
disemboweled around me were my own

—Luís Miguel Nava

I accompany the cattle hanging from their hooks.
I accompany red solitude (in bits) behind the
window pane. The bellow that (still!) splatters on
smooth stone. And the ghost of angels tattooed with
cruelty. Gluttony in transit spreads before the murmur
of the workshop of nourishing blood. That blood that
never calls forth our pity (or the instant in which the
knife sublimates our coyote half), redolent in us with
fibers of intrepid putrefaction. As if, within our inner
core, the butcher shop were standing naked stripping out
the ducts through which our sanctity comes gushing forth.

Caniboys

I

Não se matam mais humanos pra consumo,
pra fazer mingau de vísceras.

Não se matam mais em rituais
com tambores em volta da fogueira:
o olhar da presa esbugalhado
e heróis uivando para os deuses.

Matam-se pelo que não tem nome.

Mudaram-se os dígitos da insânia cíclica
no *site* da morte e sua noite metafísica.

II

O que quer um matador
em sua alma de aluguel
e seu coração de breu?

Por acaso busca o céu
ao destroçar sua presa
com a devoção de quem reza?

Por que lhe negar revanche,
ao decretar seu desmanche?

O que move um matador,
na sede que lhe sugere
a lâmina de sangue em série?

O que abisma um matador
na explosão do disparo?
Algum diamante raro?

Caniboys

I

We don't kill humans anymore to eat them,
to turn their guts into a gruel.

We don't kill them anymore in rituals
with drums around a blazing fire,
the eyes of prisoners bulging wide
and heroes howling to the gods.

We kill them for what has no name.

The digits of cyclic insanity have changed
on death's website and in its metaphysical night.

II

What does a killer want
in his rented soul,
his black hole heart?

By chance is he in search of heaven,
as he destroys his prey
with the devotion of those who pray?

Why deny his victim any second chance,
undoing him without a second glance?

What moves a killer,
in his dirty thirst, his dry-caked mud,
to seek that blade of serial blood?

What does the killer stare at
when his shots explode?
Some diamond from the mother lode?

Algum tesouro escondido
que se evola no estampido?

O que busca um matador?
Busca — por acaso — grana?
Busca, na infâmia, fama?

Acaso, a vida é o dízimo
de sua igreja de abismo?

Some hidden treasure pot
that vanishes with the shot?

What is a killer searching for?
Could it be just bucks, mere gain?
In infamy, does he seek fame?

Could it be that with his knife
he pays his church its bloody tithe?

Mangue

Despido de defesa ao que me é dano
já nem sei se me elevo ou me alucino
ou se entro — simplesmente — pelo cano
onde sonhar pareça um desatino.
A doer-me a dor tornou-me um decano
no vício da virtude em que me assino
não sei se pobre diabo ou santo insano,
seria eu — talvez — um assassino?
(…) e rolam-se os dados ao vão da sorte
ficando a vida à sanha do mais forte
e o sonho ao rés da vala e ao *bang-bang*
da usura cega e do seu passaporte.
E onde o que me cabe nesse mangue,
que planto flores quando pedem sangue?

The Swamp

Without defense against what injures me
I wonder if I've grown or gone insane,
or whether I have simply gotten in so deep
that dreaming now seems utterly in vain.
In paining me my pain makes me a dean
whose vice is claiming virtue as his own.
Am I saint or devil, or in between?
Am I a killer who is yet unknown?
(...) the dice of fortune tumble in the void
and life is left a battle of the strong
where dog eats dog and dreams of life enjoyed
with blinding greed and with its siren song.
And where do I fit in all this stinking mud,
I who plant flowers while they demand blood?

Se, Se

Para Ivan Junqueira

Se tudo que nos beija e nos acende
leva o que migra para o não sei onde
escrito numa vírgula que fende
um nome que se grita e não responde,
haveria alguma senha que resplende
dessa teia de vozes que se esconde
sabendo que o amanhã é só *the end*
sentindo que o agora já é longe?
Nada se negue ao que o viver instrui
que o fato de somar já diminui
como o voo de um pássaro que recua;
ou transeunte que, entre becos, flui
feito um bicho urbandido, um cão de rua
a farejar na lama a flor da lua.

If, If

For Ivan Junqueira

If all that kisses us and stokes our flame
will bring what migrates to the who-knows-where
carved on a comma that will rend a name
we call to without answer, in despair,
might we then watch a shining sign transcend
the weave of hidden voices without song
while knowing that tomorrow is *the end*
while feeling that today's already gone?
There's nothing to deny what living shows,
that in the very adding up we wane,
just like a bird that dwindles as it goes,
or like a man who glides through crooked lanes,
an urban stray, in search of any boon,
sniffing in mud the flower of the moon.

Nervura

Para Reynaldo Valinhos Alvarez e Moacyr Félix

Mesmo que o sangue seco nas vielas
revele o nervo exposto das sequelas

e ainda que esses canos reluzentes
(na ramagem das noites semoventes),

risquem o chão de enfermas aquarelas,
intacto o olhar ergue o mar e as velas:

algo se arrisca numa gula urgente
como um surto de amor rasgando o ventre.

São digitais do tempo os magros dias
feitos de rinhas e de epifanias;

são ritos de passagem para o nada,
ou lava de um vulcão que na calada

de um delírio maior que todo estigma,
incende a vida em sua flor de magma.

Veins

For Reynaldo Valinhos Alvarez and Moacyr Félix

Though blood may dry in darkened alleyways
it cannot hide the throbbing of our days

and even if gun barrels glistening bright
(amongst the leaves of restless, rustling night)

paint savage earth in colors sickly pale,
the gaze, intact, exalts both sea and sail:

and something pushes forward in its greed,
as might a womb, torn by its yearning need.

Fingerprints of time, lean and hungry days,
epiphanies within the daily fray;

rites of passage to utter nothingness,
or else volcanic lava that, in stillness

of fevered thoughts that rise above all stigma,
sets life afire with flaming, flowery magma.

Tulipas

O vento leste veio deitar-se
com as tulipas
no mesmo palco
em que libélulas de sangue
lampejam entre edifícios.
                    Raríssimas
vinhetas de sol
                    patinam
no esterco.

E a fúria do plasma
escrita no asfalto
torna improvável
o tempo dos idílios.

Ó placenta de narco*niños* e artefatos
de desova!
Ó lírio ensaguentado!

Por quem toca esta salva
de guizos?

Nos vultos que se erguem
do irrevogável abismo
também as palavras
                    ladram,
também os olhares ávidos
despem o ouro das manhãs
insignes.

Tulips

The east wind comes to lie
with the tulips
on the very stage
where dragonflies of blood
glitter among the buildings.
                              Rare
vignettes of sun
                  skate
surfaces of dung.

And the rage of plasma
written on asphalt
makes the coming of
an idyllic time improbable.

Oh, placenta of narcobabies and a spawn
of artifacts!
Oh, blood-soaked lilies!

For whom this tingling
salvo of applause?

With shapes that rise
from the irrevocable abyss
words as well
                  are howling
and eager gazes come to strip
away the gold of distinguished
mornings.

Lagoa

Anúncios luminosos
no espelho da lagoa

rabiscam

       na água quieta
seus liames
       voláteis.

—Ecoam fagulhas de um gestual
sincrético.

A vasta pupila
         acesa
na clausura
        lambe a noite
nua
       sob o redentor.

Lake

Luminous announcements
in the mirror of the lake

scribble

       on still water
their fleeting
       lines.

—Sparks of syncretic gestures
flowing down.

A vast pupil
        burning
in confinement
        licks the naked
night
        below the statue of the Redeemer, Christ.

Do mar 1

Para Olga Savary

Do íntimo desta noite
náutica
ouço o mar a rugir
sua língua
   ágrafa.

Vejo a lâmina,
vejo a ira,
   vejo a onda
a teimar com as pedras.

Ó perdido ancestre das águas!
Ó memória imemorial!

Despidos estão
os remos
na viva transparência,
na dança que enlaça
a terra
e desata os caminhos.

Vagam marujos
    náufragos,
velam voz
   no ermo
aos inquilinos da noite
líquida.

Sobre a córnea azulada
o tempo afia as lendas.

Ó perdido ancestre das águas!
Ó memória imemorial!

Of the Sea 1

For Olga Savary

From the intimacy of this nautical
night
I hear the sea roar
its unwritten
                    speech.

I see its surface,
I see its rage,
                    I see its wave
obstinate against the rocks.

Oh, long lost ancestor of waters!
Oh, memory immemorial!

Naked are
the oars
in bright transparency,
in a dance that enchants
the earth
and unleashes its paths.

Shipwrecked mariners
                    drift about,
and voices sail
                    through the wilderness
to tenants of the liquid
night.

Over the bluish cornea
time hones its tales.

Oh, long lost ancestor of waters!
Oh, memory immemorial!

Êxtase

Dançam hibiscos
na fotografia
dançam
sem movimento
absortos
em sua rubra
caligrafia
dançam hibiscos
de sangue
dançam na íris
da cidade
dançam no clima
dançam na rima
dançam no olho
da fotografia
dançam no cromo
do dia
dançam exóticos
dançam exatos
extasiados
no estático
dançam
dançam

dão-se.

Ecstasy

Hibiscuses dance
in the photograph
they dance
motionless
absorbed
in their crimson
calligraphy
hibiscuses of blood
they dance
they dance in the eyes
of the city
they dance these climes
they dance these rhymes
they dance in the eye
of the photograph
they dance lithe lithograph
of day
they dance exotic
they dance exact
in ecstasy
statically
they dance
they dance

they ~~surrender.~~ yield
to dance.

ORNAMENTS FOR AN ECLIPSE

(Adereços para um Eclipse)

Il s'agit pour moi de faire parler les choses…

—Francis Ponge

Persona

(...) e o que de nós transmigra
para o que não é palavra
e forma,
o que é informe
e ter sido
sob o solstício e o vento
sem legenda.
E no entanto lume
no verbo escarnado
sob a cesura que se esgarça
ao indefinível.
E no entanto é nome,
persona,
hologramas no vácuo
que são sem o Ser.

Persona

(…) and what transmigrates from us
to what is neither word
nor form,
the unformed
that was
beneath the solstice and the wind
without a legend.
And nonetheless a flame
in the word stripped of flesh
beneath a caesura fading
toward the indefinable.
And nonetheless it is name,
persona,
a hologram in the void
that is without Being.

O ouro das coisas

Para Luís Augusto Cassas

Daqui desses becos
                    absolutos
luta-se
        no fórum
do lítero,
onde o reles relativo
transcende
            seus delitos.
Daqui destes estames (tramem
o Samadhi-ser:
o nada náufrago
sob o Nadalume)

amanhece.

E quilhas vazam marés
                        aqui
deste Ashramaxé:
                    imaginário
templo
        de amaravilhas.

Que a palavra solavanque
o ouro das dez mil coisas.

The Gold in Things

For Luís Augusto Cassas

From these absolute
                    byways
there is a battle
                    in the courtroom
of the literous,
where the contemptible relative
transcends
              its crimes.
From these threads (they weave
the Samadhi-Being:
the nothing castaway
beneath the Nothingflame)

comes the dawn.

And keels carve the tides
                          here
in this Ashramaxé:*
                     imaginary
temple
      of the amarvelous.

May the word jolt
the gold of ten thousand things.

* Neologism made of Ashram and *axé*, Brazilian word for energy derived from the Yoruba

Litania Leiga

Para Nise da Silveira

Venho ao mar de memória, irmã
—a mão timbrada em gestos—
esculpir teus dias íngremes
sob o vento oblíquo.

Venho a ti
para quem o estigma
é *anima*.

A ti
que viste a cor do inconsciente.

Ainda sangram digitais
do século findo
sobre teus insanos sãos.

Com rasura,
fomos salvos pela loucura.

E onde fores vai—
não a ira—a íris
do olhar dos gatos.

Agora, escuta.
Agora que és de magma
e lumes.
Escuta esta litania leiga
deserta sob as palavras.

Agora que retornas
ao silêncio *in natura*.

Layman's Litany

For Nise da Silveira*

I approach the sea of memory, my sister
—hand crested with gestures—
to sculpt your steep days
beneath the slanting wind.

I come to you
for whom stigma
is *anima.*

To you
who saw the color of the unconscious.

Last century's fingerprints
are bleeding still
upon your salvaged lunatics.

Obliterated,
we were saved by madness.

And wherever you might go—
not ire—but the irises
of staring cats were there.

Listen to me now.
Now that you are magma
and luminous.
Listen to this layman's litany
alone, beyond all words.

Now that you return
to silence *in natura.*

* Renowned Brazilian disciple of Jung, who founded the practice of art therapy

Mater

Fico aqui debaixo destas palmeiras, assuntando o tempo,
recebendo a mensalidade das plantas.
— Dona Raimunda Salgado

I

De ti não há sequer
um álbum de família:
retratos da infância
nos campos de arroz e gergelim.

Talvez reste em pensamento
pedaços de tua voz
                    no vento
como impressões digtais
num rio.

II

No dia em que o azul
roubou teus olhos
e o silêncio rival rasgou
teu nome,
cotovias cantaram no meu rastro.
No dia em que a manhã
cerrou teus olhos.

III

Sem ti
sou a flor da árvore
desolada. Agora
o mar bate em minhas rochas
e a noite ronda meus calcanhares.

Mater

*Sometimes I sit under one of those palms, taking in the wind
and the monthly payments of the plants.*

— Dona Raimunda Salgado

I

Of you there's ~~nothing but~~ *not even*
a family album:
photos of childhood
in fields of rice and sesame.

Maybe in my thoughts there linger
fragments of your voice
                              in the wind
like fingerprints
on a river.

II

On the day the blue
stole your eyes
and silence tore apart
your name,
skylarks started singing in my tracks.
On the day the morning
closed your eyes.

III

Without you
I am the blossom on the tree,
bereft. Now
the sea beats against my rocks
and the night prowls at my heels.

Ladainha

Para Mestre Wu

Somente a música (íntima)
da noite
seguiu mestre Wu
ao jardim das flores amarelas.

Da terra-mater
seu ímã vital fundiu-se aos astros.

Resoluto,
como um rio se despe ao mar.

Sobre nós permanecem
as palavras inéditas
e a dor das coisas relativas.

O resto cabe ao silêncio
que cinge o tempo ao não tempo.

Litany

For Master Wu

Only the (intimate) music
of the night
followed Master Wu
to the garden of yellow flowers.

From *terra mater*
his vital magnet melded with the stars.

Resolute,
the way a river strips naked for the sea.

Over us remain
unspoken words
and the pain of relative things.

The rest fits within silence
tying time to non-time.

Faíscas

Faíscas sutis emanam
dos objetos frios, insólitos.

Secretas impressões incidem
feito ranhuras no osso:

o malho da mão no lapso provisório.

Dispersos em toda parte insistem
os inutensílios a nos assediar:

arrulham no sopro que acorda as coisas
mudas.

Sparks

Subtle sparks emanate
from objects cold and strange.

Secret impressions advance
like grooves in bone:

the hand's work in the slippage of time.

Scattered everywhere, non-utensils
importune us:

they murmur in the breath that awakens speechless
things.

Corolário

Para Claudia Roquette-Pinto

As pétalas rebeldes
— no infinito branco —
uivam silêncios, respingam
onde o espinho suja o verso; ou
fulminam (rítmicas)
para dentro da veia
— vilãs: as pétalas fulgurantes
como o olho azul na rocha
lacerada. E ramagens
sincréticas de palárvores-flor
se despetalam
                    — devolutas.

No estribo do vívido verbo
o coração — acossado —
rruge
        em seu coice de plumas.

Corollary

For Claudia Roquette-Pinto

Rebellious petals
—in a white infinity—
howl silences, splatter
where thorn soils verse; or
flare (rhythmic)
within the vein
—villains: petals sparkling
like blue eyes in a lacerated
rock. And syncretic
branching whirl-whorled words
shed their petals
                                —broken free.

In the stirrup of the vibrant verb
the heart—harassed and cornered—
rroars
        its feathered thud.

Bilro

Para Adriano Espínola

No bilro—em conta-gotas percussivo
como num fio de orvalho rutilante—
enreda-se a rendeira, em gesto altivo,
como se o voo das mãos dissesse: cante!
E diz, no labirinto remissivo
de linhas que se cruzam conflitantes
pelo refrão de outro tear-arquivo,
que o tempo descostura a cada instante:
o coração, que em sua tecelagem
de ritmos e reveses leva à estiagem
o sopro da existência e sua lenda,
num fluir secreto e com tal voltagem,
que o que se tece já não é a renda,
é a própria vida que se desemenda.

The Bobbin

For Adriano Espínola

On the bobbin — percussive drops of time
that fall as from a dew-bright glistening string —
the lace-entangled lace maker sublime,
as if her flying hands were saying: sing!
And so they say, in labyrinthine lines
that lead us crisscross and against the grain
to conflict with our archive loom's refrain,
that loom's work fraying steadily with time:
our heart, that always in its onward weave
of rhythm and reverses leads toward drought
the breath of life, the myths that we believe,
the secret flow, the force that does not doubt.
And so what's being woven isn't lace,
but life itself unweaving into space.

Arma Zen

Para João Manuel Lima Mira

Na pintura de Musachi o arbusto pendura o voo
do pássaro. Vívidos na moldura (arbusto e pássaro),
imovem-se na constante impermanência.
(Também no rito da esgrima *zen* o voo da mão na
empunhadura enluva a lâmina e o samurai.)
Morte. Tempo. Vida e Via fundem-se no corte.
Que de tão ágil é *não agir.*

Zenarm

For João Manuel Lima Mira

In Musachi's painting the bush suspends the bird's flight.
Vivid in their frame (bush and bird), they remain motionless in
permanent impermanence. (As in the rite of zen fencing the
flight of the hand on the hilt envelops blade and samurai.)
Death. Time. Life and The Way merge in the stroke.
Agile beyond action.

Tigre de Origami

Para Alice K.

Límpido o papel em branco
ladra (sob o tempo quântico),

as nossas rasuras raras,
desamares, mãos avaras,

lavas de sangue (e bem mais
que esta babel de fonemas

—incisa de vãs verdades—
arde), ao clã de veleidades

onde 1+1 não são dois
nem o verbo rege a luz,

pois o mundo às vezes teme
que a palavra se apoeme.

E se o monitor delata
o papel fora de pauta,

límpida a lauda—em seu nada—
soletra o silêncio, alada

ao caos. Nem fogo dispersa,
nem água é algo que impeça,

que num átimo ela se arme
em um tigre de origami.

Origami Tiger

For Alice K.

The blank page without a line
growls (beneath quantum time),

our carved up scars,
our marred and hardened hearts,

a bloody lava flow (lots more aflame
than that babel of phonemes

—sliced through with vanities *en masse*—)
fronting vast futilities of class

where 1+1 makes 2 is not quite right
and where the Word does not create the light,

for the world, at times, fears the curse
of the word that may turn into verse.

And if the modern monitor
denounces paper as a dinosaur

the blank page—in its nullity—
spells out silence in proximity

to chaos. And fire cannot scatter,
nor can water splatter

to prevent it turning to a bright
origami tiger in the night.

Sinergia

Para Sebastião Uchoa Leite

Escrita ascética (quase sem palavras)
visando a sinergia do signo

(o drible dança à borda
na linha do gol olímpico)

Escrita cítrica, exata:
rímel de ouro sobre a pauta

Pinçadas ao papel as palavras
(sem alarde) falam

diamante: o raio sem a pedra.

Synergy

For Sebastião Uchoa Leite

Ascetic script (almost without words)
seeking synergy with its sign

(The dribble dances on the edge
the perfect base-line goal).

Citric script, exact:
golden mascara on a blank sheet.

Placed precise on paper, words
(without bravado) speak

a diamond's brilliance without the stone.

Adereços para um eclipse

I

As joias rituais
de Liliana Reyes O.
reinam na entranha
do vívido transe.
Ínfimas relíquias
de metal
      laboram
na fibra orgânica
miragens de ancestres
                vivos
— e extintos.

São plumas terçando prata
são pétalas de ouro e zênite.

II

Os fósseis ganham
             asas,
secretas razões de alento,
que em plumas
descerram
       vestes,
vórtices.

Linhas de interlúnios
e acalantos
que enredam rendas
          de relâmpagos.

III

Nuns, a *madera encendida*
hospeda ouro em cartuchos;

Ornaments for an Eclipse

I

The ritual jewels
of Lilian Reyes O.*
reign in the entrails
of vibrant trance.
Minute mementos
in metal
            toil
within organic fibers
specters of ancestors
                        living
—and dead.

They are feathers silver-interlaced
they are petals of zenith and of gold.

II

Fossils grow
            wings,
secret cause for encouragement,
that in feathers
disclose
            vestments,
vortices.

Interlunar lines
and lullabies
that enlace the lace
                        of lightning bolts.

III

'Nsome, *madera encendida***
hosts gold in cartridges;

* Colombian sculptress who creates small objects using
  materials and motifs from pre-Colombian art
** Spanish for "wood in flames"

noutros,
estames de prata e luz
aderem ao quartzo.

(Múltiplas alusões de linhas
curvas
          interpretam mitos.)

E ogivas de plumas raras
formam casulos
nunsoutros.

IV

O fervilhar da alquimia
de elementais
que acessa vozes a submissas
leis

          despe sob a íris
o gesto em objeto.
Tanto
que do árido solo dos metais
transbordam sóis
desatam lãs.

V

Dançam pássaros da memória
no dorso da terra lúbrica

trazem no bico gerânios
trazem nas asas a música

da noite que tange as lendas
aos rios de seixo e prata

tecem a nova oferenda
no que restou dos piratas.

in others,
stalks of silver and light
adhere to quartz.

(Multiple allusions of curved
lines
        whisper myths.)

And warheads of rare feathers
form cocoons
'nsomeothers.

IV

The boiling of the alchemy
of elements
that seeks out voices for submissive
laws

        unveils beneath our eyes
the gesture turned to object.
So much so
that from the arid soil of metals
suns overflow
and fleece is freed.

V

Birds of memory dance
on the back of lubricious earth

They bring in their beaks geraniums
they bring on their wings the music

of night that relegates legends
to rivers of silver and stone

they weave a new-made offering
from pirate detritus and bone.

Yanomami

Para Sapain e Américo Peret

Quando vierem os filhos
do mênstruo
com suas línguas de pólvora,
quando vierem as hordas
rudes,

chama Tupã
chama Xamã

Quando vier a luz sangrenta,
quando vierem os deuses homicidas
com sua sede de pedras,

chama Tupã
chama Xamã

Quando os lugares sagrados
forem tocados a noite virá!
Virá como o hálito da manhã
pois estarei me pondo
fraco;

a noite virá como o vento
pois estarei morrendo:

quando o rio grifar
na terra ácida
sua legenda de sangue.

Ó vento que alinha o destino!
Ó rito que fala os ancestres!

chama Tupã
chama Xamã.

Yanomami

For Sapain and Américo Peret

When the children of menstruation
come
with gunpowder tongues,
when the barbarous hordes
come,

call Tupã
call Xamã

When the bloody light comes,
the homicidal gods
with their thirst for stones,

Call Tupã
Call Xamã

When the sacred places
are disturbed night will come!
It will come like the breath of morning
for I will be growing
weak;

The night will come like the wind
for I will be dying:

when the river carves
from bitter earth
its legend of blood.

Oh wind that aligns our destiny!
Oh rite that speaks to our ancestors!

Call Tupã
Call Xamã.

Odu

Para Hilda Dias dos Santos

No corpo do elegún
os deuses descem ao sangue súplice.
Retornam ao sal dos vivos.

Os deuses em sua névoa incorpórea.

Retornam da secreta paisagem
do não tempo.

No vão do sem forma
tambores percutem a voz das sombras.

Odu

For Hilda Dias dos Santos

In the body of the *elegún**
the gods descend to supplicating blood.
They return to the salt of the living.

The gods in their incorporeal mists.

They return from a secret countryside
of non-time.

In the void of formlessness
drums beat out the shadow's voice.

* Yoruba word for the body of a person that receives a spirit

Tinta forte

Estou ruído na carne,
não no símbolo
que é de pedra
e pégaso.

Andaimes de mim
se erguem
sob uma febre
                  onírica
que da memória
                  esplende
aos ossos
e aos glóbulos.

Estou no gume
e basta
o que se alastra
às veias
          e seu esquivo ouro.

Meu rito avança
sobre a linfa.

(Inda que da saga
férrea
        se emoldure
ao couro
a senha do curtume
                          fero.)

Na dor
o real
        desce
ao osso
cru
e esgarçado
como o avesso
a ver-
        se.

Deepest Black

I am gnawed away in flesh
not in a symbol
made of stone
and Pegasus.

Scaffolds rise
from me
beneath a dream
                    fever
that from memory
                    radiates resplendent
to the bones
and corpuscles.

I'm on the razor edge
and what spreads
to my veins
                    and their fleeting gold
suffices.

My rite floods
through my lymph.

(Even if from the brutish
saga
        they are stamping out
the stigma of
cruel tanned
                    skins.)

In pain
the real
                descends
to the bone
raw
and splintered
like the inside
gazing at it
                    self.

As horas
        em sépia
derrotam o cerco
da promessa
tal que do excesso
—essência.

E nem o tenro
                ser
da água
        em módulos
muda
a dor que dói
no sangue
a dor
no impalpável.

O magma da raça
infenso
        ao mangue
transluz
        da canga
                bruta:
lavas de sol
primal
renga de tambor
tribal
cateretê
babá.

Árduo de transe
e (extrema)
                espera
desespero
num *rap* réptil
num latir
        de latas
reino

à flor da pele
da tinta forte
em que me negam.

Hours
      in sepia
defeat the circling
of promise
so that from the excess
—essence.

And not even the tender
                being
of water
      in modules
changes
the pain that pains
the blood
the pain
of the impalpable.

The magma of the race
hostile
      to the mango marsh
erupts
      from the brute
             yoke:
lava of primeval
sun
renga of the tribal
drum
cateretê
babá.

Ardent in trance
and the (endless)
          wait
desperate
in a reptile rap
the tin can
      yap
I reign

on the surface of my flesh
of deepest black
where they deny me.

Coda

Para Ferreira Gullar

Agora que cantar é flor
de lavas, lides
e o sol sanguíneo raia
nosso cais,
uma foz de lábios
nos incesta ao arbítrio
antes que rapinas raptem
nosso último grão de víscera.

Cantar como as pedras rolam
cantar como o sangue cinge
os dígitos do amor mensurável.

Radical amanhece
a ramagem de incêndios
sobre as vinhas.

Do sublime à barbárie
eis que o destino inscreve-se
nos dentes.

Transidos recolhemos a penugem
do sol
     e o silêncio
em riste.

No ermo do ter-se sem se pertencer
só o impermanente permanece.

Coda

For Ferreira Gullar

Now that singing is lava's flower
the struggle of life
and the blood of the sun cast rays
upon our quay,
a river mouth of lips
joins in incest with our will
before raptors ravage
the last grain from our guts.

To sing the way stones roll
to sing the way blood binds
the digits of a love defined.

Implacable, the foliage
of conflagrations
over the vineyards dawns.

From the sublime to the barbaric,
see how destiny is carved
into our teeth.

Possessed we harvest the down
of sun
        and silence
with its warning finger.

In the solitude of being without belonging
only the impermanent endures.

Afterword
Luiz Fernando Valente

The publication of *Blood of the Sun (Sol Sangüíneo)* is the felicitous outcome of a spectacular collaboration between one of the most influential and innovative contemporary Brazilian poets and one of the most accomplished English language translators from the Portuguese. I am honored to be a godfather of sorts to this stunning new volume, as I had the pleasure of bringing Salgado Maranhão and Alexis Levitin together during "A Moveable Feast," a festival of poetry in Portuguese, held at Brown University in the spring of 2007. That introduction was far from fortuitous. I had known and worked with Alexis since the early 1980s, and had always been impressed by the combination of precision, elegance, and creativity displayed in his superb translations from the Portuguese, both in prose and in verse. I had also been an early admirer and, indeed, the first person in the United States to have taught and written about Salgado's poetry. I believed that it was high time Salgado's work became available to English language audiences. And I was convinced that only a translator with deep sensitivity to the nuances of *both* Portuguese and English poetic language would be able to do justice to the intricate syntax and imagery that is the hallmark of Salgado's poetry.

It is important to clarify from the outset that in underscoring the intricacy of Salgado's poetic language, by no means am I suggesting that Salgado's poetry is formalist or hermetic or primarily about language games. Rather, Salgado Maranhão is an unabashed humanist, in whose poetry converge a range of universal feelings, emotions, and quests—love, loss, pain, desire, loneliness, generosity, brutality, longing, sensuality, sexuality—while dialoguing with the best in the Luso-Brazilian poetic canon—Camões, Pessoa, Drummond, Cabral, and Faustino, among others. For Salgado, form is never gratuítous. As Salgado Maranhão and Geraldo Carneiro stated in their joint 2009 manifesto "The Uncommandments" ("Os Desmandamentos," trans. Alexis Levitin),

> For us poets the problem isn't just to make
> poetry well-constructed, but to make it distinct
> (in the double sense, implying both difference

and elegance). It is an exercise that is vital for
maintaining the vigor of the word. Poetry is not
just a question of truth, but of ecstasy. That's why
we are poets of ecstasy: the ecstasy of language,
the ecstasy of life.

Borrowing from Mark Schorer's influential essay, we could say
that Salgado's poetry exemplifies "Technique as Discovery."
There is an inextricable correlation between Salgado's intricate
poetic language and the poet's readiness to delve into the
deepest and most paradoxical layers of being, in a never-
ending struggle with the mystery of human existence in an
often-indifferent world. Salgado's poetry is "difficult" because
it boldly tackles difficult issues and asks difficult questions.
Rather than pretend that it can be an unmediated expression
of individual feelings, Salgado's poetry is a highly crafted
invitation for the reader to join in a labyrinthine process of
reflection and questioning. Indeed, Salgado's poetic diction
could be said to resonate with the following marvelous lines by
Galician poet Chus Pato (1955---): "language is a labyrinth of
pathways / traffic" ("a linguaxe é un labirinto de camiños / un
tráfico"). The history of mythology teaches us that the labyrinth
was an elaborate structure, constructed by that greatest of all
artificers, Daedalus. Moreover, in our time, the labyrinth has
become a commonly used image for the anomie, silence, and
loss of self that are often associated with the modern human
condition, and with much modernist and post-modernist
literature. As is the case with Pato, however, the "labyrinth
of pathways" that lies at the foundation of Salgado's poetry
embodies a refusal to be silenced, that is, a refusal to capitulate
to the so-called modern condition. In other words, it stands for
resistance against, rather than surrender to the dehumanizing
forces of modernity.

In this sense, Salgado's poetry exemplifies the
transformative function of literature, while assuming an
intrinsically mediating, liminal quality. Salgado's poems may
start with the most commonplace objects from the quotidian,
but they allow us to glimpse something that wasn't there at the

outset, the kind of "terceira margem," or "third bank," evoked in Guimarães Rosa's archetypical short story "The Third Bank of the River." As suggested by the epigraph from Francis Ponge to the section "Ornaments for an Eclipse" ("Adereços para um Eclipse") in *Blood of the Sun*, for Salgado, as for his French counterpart, "it is a matter of making things speak" ("il s'agit pour moi de faire parler les choses"). At this point it would be useful to return to Salgado Maranhão and Geraldo Carneiro's words in "The Uncommandments": "that there be space for and faith in poetry. And that it continue to manufacture futures and, like phoenix, destroy and reconstruct itself for all eternity and one more day." Rather than merely representing or celebrating outside reality, Salgado's poetry stands on what could be described as an exhilarating *threshold of possibility*.

In keeping with the concept of poetry as a threshold, the third section of the volume consists of a cycle of six poems, which, in a way or another, call into question the artificial dividing line between supposed contraries. Significantly, though the individual poems are titled "Boundary 1–7" ("Limítrofe 1–7"), the title of the section is "Loom of Feeling" ("Tear dos Afetos"). The metaphor of weaving is appropriate. Just as a beautifully woven piece of material obscures, in the harmony of the final product, the original tension between the warp and the weft, a successful poem supersedes the myriad threads of feelings and emotions, which make up our complex and often contradictory existence. The epigraph from René Char that opens the section that follows "Loom of Feeling," titled "Gray Legend" ("Legenda Gris"), serves as a clue leading to such an interpretation of the "Boundary" poems: "who's the man of the morning, and who's the one of darkness?" ("Lequel est l'homme du matin et lequel celui des ténèbres?").

In fact, many of the poems in *Blood of the Sun* call into question the system of binary oppositions with which the western tradition has attempted to impose order on the world. Most notable among them is the opposition between the body and the spirit, or, put differently, between the inferior flesh and the superior mind, which Salgado's poetry rejects. Though a diffuse, Zenlike spirituality permeates Salgado's poetry, many poems remind us that ultimately and inevitably as human beings we are our bodies—but rather than a limitation or constraint, the body may be a source of liberation. That our humanity is framed by the materiality of our bodies, rather than the abstraction of our souls, is suggested by the very title of the collection, *Sol Sangüíneo*—or *Blood of the Sun*, in Levitin's marvelous rendition—which imagines even inanimate nature as possessing a "body."

This is not, however, the same as envisaging poetry as the mere expression of the individual. The best lyric poetry is never an immediate outpouring of the poet's subjectivity but a more profound sounding—embodied in the case of Salgado's poetry in the recurring image of magma—of the relationship between being and the world, mediated by images. Salgado's poetry yearns to take us to a dimension where we may be able to see things in reverse and the usual oppositions may be transcended.

Although I have been emphasizing the existential and aesthetic dimensions of resistance in Salgado's poetry, *Blood of the Sun* also deals with resistance in a social, political, and historical way. In this sense the present volume modulates an important facet of Salgado's poetry since he first came into the literary scene as a participant of the 1978 anthology *Rage to Right: Thirteen Impossible Poets (Ebulição da Escrivatura: Treze Poetas Impossíveis)*, published at the very moment when questions of race and gender began to be more openly discussed in Brazil, while the country embarked on a path to full redemocratization, the gradual, ten-year-long process known as the *abertura*. Salgado's universal humanism by no means whitewashes the poet's concrete situation as an Afro-Brazilian man. Racial and historical issues are not marginal concerns, but instead constitute an intrinsic element of his poetry and worldview. In fact, in the long first poem of the collection, entitled "Blood of the Sun (Flat Lands)" ("Sol Sangüíneo (Terra chã)"), a *summa* of the themes that will be developed in the volume, the poet boldly states that "my home is my skin" ("minha terra é minha pele"), and proceeds to evoke the history of subjugation and discrimination to which he is inescapably linked. Being Black is an unavoidable mark of distinction, understood here as difference, but also a badge of honor. In "Deepest Black" ("Tinta forte"), the poet combines a poignant lament for the historical oppression of people of African descent with defiant pride in their African heritage.

Nevertheless, Salgado's personal history as a Black man is inseparable from his larger concern that any inhumane action detracts from our collective humanity and diminishes us all as human beings. There are other examples in the volume: the strong feelings of disgust and fear evoked by the drawing of a swastika on a wall in the poem ironically titled "Mural"; the jeremiad against the genocide of indigenous people in "Yanomami"; the dirge for pre-Columbian culture in "Ornaments for an Eclipse" ("Adereços para um Eclipse").

Influenced by Zen Buddhism, Salgado's poetry conveys a calm acceptance of the paradoxes of being human, as revealed, among others, in "Rage" ("Fero"): "Nothing ransoms me. / Am I the killer / or the killed?" ("Nada me resgata. / Não sei se sou quem morre / ou quem mata."); or in "Limítrofe 7" ("Boundary 7"): "Before what suffers / and what sleeps / just dust / and reticence" ("Ante o que dói / e o que dorme: / apenas pó / e reticências"); or in "Coda": "In the solitude of being without belonging / only the impermanent endures" ("No ermo de ter-se sem se pertencer / só o impermanente permanece"). In Salgado's view, even if the raw material of poetry is transience and impermanence, from fleeting time to our mortal bodies, combined with the pervasiveness of suffering, loss and cruelty, embodied in such images as *magma, lavas,* and *lama,* the aesthetic experience, defying all odds, can bring us at least to a more lucid and generous understanding of our common humanity. It is in this sense that art becomes a "Zen weapon," or "Zenarm" in Levitin's translation, ("Arma Zen") and the poem may metamorphose into an "Origami Tiger" ("Tigre de Origami"). For, ultimately, poetry's main achievement is to bring us back home to the origins of the word, and as such, to our own origins as human beings.

Luiz Fernando Valente is Professor of Portuguese and Brazilian Studies and Comparative Literature at Brown University.

Translator's Note
Alexis Levitin

Working with Salgado Maranhão on this translation was an enormous pleasure. Salgado's English is limited, but he has a deep sense of music and is alive to the melodic otherness of the English language. Our collaboration involved a great deal of reading aloud of both the original and the translation. Salgado's poetic voice is a kind of mesmerizing song-chant he learned as a child listening to his mother recite *literatura de Cordel,* a popular form of poetry practiced by traveling modern-day troubadours. My task was to listen attentively to his voice. He would then listen to mine. Our final decisions were often based on the sound rather than mere lexical fidelity. We agreed that the greatest fidelity had to be to the music of the poetry itself. So, if the bilingual reader discovers some liberties in the text, especially in heavily rhymed poems, be assured that they were agreed to by the poet himself for the sake of sound, the deepest truth in language.

I would like to express my great gratitude to Luiz Fernando Valente, Chair of the Department of Portuguese and Brazilian Studies at Brown University for bringing Salgado and me together. It was his belief in this project that got us started and kept us going. I would also like to thank my friend and fellow translator Wayne Miller, who gave the entire translation a meticulous and wise reading. Thanks also to SUNY-Plattsburgh for a travel grant to Brazil that enabled me to work with Salgado on his adopted home turf of Rio de Janeiro. Thanks also to Carlos Dimuro, Iracy Souza, and Valeria Gauz in Brazil for their kind assistance with proofreading the original text. Last but not least, I would like to thank Daniel Slager and all the friendly and helpful folk at Milkweed Editions.

Salgado Maranhão's *A Cor da Palavra (The Color of the Word)* was named the best book of poetry by the Brazilian Academy of Letters in 2011. An earlier collection, *Mural de Ventos (Mural of Winds)*, won the prestigious Prêmio Jabuti in 1999. In addition to his nine books of poetry, Maranhão has written song lyrics and made recordings with some of Brazil's leading jazz and pop musicians. *Sol Sangüíneo (Blood of the Sun)* is Maranhão's first book to appear in English translation.

Alexis Levitin has translated thirty-one books, mostly from the Portuguese, including Clarice Lispector's *Soulstorm* and Eugénio de Andrade's *Forbidden Words*. His most recent books are a co-translation of *Tapestry of the Sun: An Anthology of Ecuadorian Poetry,* the first anthology of Ecuadorian poetry to be published in English, and *A Traveler's Literary Companion to Brazil.* He is a Distinguished Professor at SUNY-Plattsburgh.

Milkweed Editions

Founded as a nonprofit organization in 1980, Milkweed Editions is an independent publisher. Our mission is to identify, nurture and publish transformative literature, and build an engaged community around it.

Join Us

In addition to revenue generated by the sales of books we publish, Milkweed Editions depends on the generosity of institutions and individuals like you. In an increasingly consolidated and bottom-line-driven publishing world, your support allows us to select and publish books on the basis of their literary quality and transformative potential. Please visit our Web site (www.milkweed.org) or contact us at (800) 520-6455 to learn more.

Milkweed Editions, a nonprofit publisher, gratefully acknowledges sustaining support from the following:

Maurice and Sally Blanks
Emilie and Henry Buchwald
The Bush Foundation
The Patrick and Aimee Butler
 Foundation
Timothy and Tara Clark
Betsy and Edward Cussler
The Dougherty Family Foundation
Mary Lee Dayton
Julie B. DuBois
Fundação Biblioteca Nacional
Joanne and John Gordon
Ellen Grace
William and Jeanne Grandy
John and Andrea Gulla
Elizabeth Driscoll Hlavka and Edwin
 Hlavka
The Jerome Foundation
The Lerner Foundation
The Lindquist & Vennum Foundation
Sanders and Tasha Marvin
Robert E. and Vivian McDonald
The McKnight Foundation
Mid-Continent Engineering
The Minnesota State Arts Board,
 through an appropriation by
 the Minnesota State Legislature
 and a grant from the National
 Endowment for the Arts
Christine and John L. Morrison
Kelly Morrison and John Willoughby
The National Endowment for the Arts
Ann and Doug Ness

Jörg and Angie Pierach
The RBC Foundation USA
Deborah Reynolds
Cheryl Ryland
Schele and Philip Smith
The Target Foundation
The Travelers Foundation
Moira Turner
Edward and Jenny Wahl

ART WORKS.
arts.gov

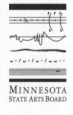

CLEAN WATER LAND & LEGACY AMENDMENT

MINNESOTA STATE ARTS BOARD

BUSH FOUNDATION

TARGET.

Interior design and typesetting
by Hopkins/Baumann
Printed on acid-free 100% postconsumer waste paper
by Friesens Corporation

ENVIRONMENTAL BENEFITS STATEMENT

Milkweed Editions saved the following resources by printing the pages of this book on chlorine free paper made with 100% post-consumer waste.

TREES	WATER	ENERGY	SOLID WASTE	GREENHOUSE GASES
24	11,302	10	718	2,506
FULLY GROWN	GALLONS	MILLION BTUs	POUNDS	POUNDS

Environmental impact estimates were made using the Environmental Paper Network Paper Calculator. For more information visit www.papercalculator.org.